HEROES OF HISTORY FOR YOUNG READERS
ACTIVITY GUIDE
FOR BOOKS 1-4

George Washington • Meriwether Lewis
Clara Barton • George Washington Carver

Renee Taft Meloche

 Emerald Books

P.O. BOX 635
LYNNWOOD, WA 98046

Emerald Books are distributed through YWAM Publishing. For a full list of titles, including other great activity guides, visit our website at www.ywampublishing.com or call 1-800-922-2143.

Heroes of History for Young Readers Activity Guide for Books 1–4
Copyright © 2007 by Renee Meloche

12 11 10 09 08 07   10 9 8 7 6 5 4 3 2 1

Published by Emerald Books
P.O. Box 635
Lynnwood, Washington 98046

ISBN-10: 1-932096-47-7
ISBN-13: 978-1-932096-47-7

Printed in the United States of America.

Contents

Introduction

This activity guide is designed to accompany the following books from the Heroes of History for Young Readers series by Renee Taft Meloche and Bryan Pollard: *George Washington: America's Patriot; Meriwether Lewis: Journey Across America; Clara Barton: Courage to Serve;* and *George Washington Carver: America's Scientist.* It provides the schoolteacher and homeschooling parent with ways to teach and reinforce the important lessons of these books.

The guide contains the following parts for each hero:

* **Coloring Page.** There is a picture of each hero with memorable people and events surrounding him or her for the children to color.
* **Hero Song.** The hero song is a tool to reinforce the main lesson of the hero. Music is often more memorable than spoken or written text.
* **Character Quality.** Each hero is given a character quality for the children to focus on. Discussion questions and visual aids are provided.
* **Character Activity.** The character activities use drama or arts and crafts to convey more fully the character quality of the hero.
* **Character Song.** The character song encourages children to develop the particular character quality in their own lives.
* **Shoebox Activity.** This activity uses arts and crafts to create a keepsake to remember each hero and what they accomplished. The children will put this keepsake into a shoebox (or other container) so that they will have a treasure box of memories of the heroes.
* **Cultural Page.** This page illustrates something that is representative of the people each hero worked among, such as an animal, game, craft, or recipe.
* **Map.** The children will color a map relevant to the hero's life.
* **Flag.** A flag is provided for the children to color.
* **Fact Quiz.** This page tests the children's comprehension of each hero story by giving true and false statements inside a particular object that relates to that story. The children will color in the true statements and draw an X over the false statements.
* **Fun with Rhyme.** This page has six stanzas from each hero story. The last word of each stanza is blank, and the children try to fill in the blank, rhyming it with the last word in the second line. A Word Bank is provided for very young readers. (When making copies, the Word Bank can be covered up for the more advanced reader and speller.)
* **Crossword Puzzle.** This page tests the children's comprehension of each story. A Word Bank is provided for young readers. (Again, when making copies, the Word Bank can be covered up.)
* **Can You Name the Hero?** This exercise has four stanzas, each providing clues about a hero. The children guess which hero each stanza is about.

Before you begin this activity guide, you may want to highlight which activities best suit your needs. For instance, a schoolteacher might want to focus more on the crossword puzzle, fact, map, and cultural pages than on the songs and coloring pages. A thirteen-week syllabus is included at the end of this activity guide for those parents and teachers who would like a guide to covering some or all of the activities.

Reinforcing stories with fun and creative illustrations, songs, drama, and arts and crafts brings the heroes to life and helps children remember the important lessons learned through the lives of heroes—ordinary men and women who did extraordinary things in history.

George Washington: America's Patriot

George Washington Song

George Washington led hungry, tired men through freezing storms until Great Britain gave up and America was born.

George bravely led the colonists to independence; then as president, America chose him to lead again.

First hero, first hero, America's first hero. George led the fight for liberty so we can all live free.

First hero, first hero, America's first hero. First president—George Washington—a great American.

The Good Character Quality
of George Washington

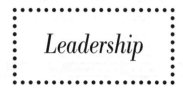

Leadership

Definition of Leadership: The ability to motivate and inspire.

Steps to Follow

1. Introduce the character quality of leadership, which describes George, and discuss its meaning with the children.

2. Ask the children, "How did George show leadership in his life through his words or actions?"
    - ❖ As colonel for the British army, he led his men for three years until the French lost the war.
    - ❖ As general, George led sixteen thousand men from thirteen different colonies to defend themselves against the British.
    - ❖ George led his men in driving the British out of Boston so effectively that the British had to hire Hessian soldiers from Germany.
    - ❖ Even though George's men were tired and freezing, he led them on a daring surprise raid on the Hessians' camp.
    - ❖ George led his men so successfully that Great Britain finally surrendered in 1781.
    - ❖ George wisely led his country for eight years as the first president of the United States.

3. Have the children sing the character song "We Will Be Great Leaders" on page 11. (This song is sung to the tune of "Do Your Ears Hang Low?" If you have the CD for George Washington, you can have the children follow or sing along with this song. At the end of the CD, there is a solo piano accompaniment that the children can sing along with as well.)

George Washington Character Song
We Will Be Great Leaders

We will be great lead - ers who'll al - ways do our best to lead oth - ers by our ex - am - ple, yes! We will be great lead - ers and al - ways pave the way in our lives each day.

Character Activity for George Washington
Showing Leadership

Materials

- ❖ Music with a strong beat
- ❖ A piece of paper listing six different actions, such as *fall, freeze, run, sit, walk, turn*
- ❖ A piece of paper listing ten different actions, such as *clap, crawl, cry, dance, hop, roll over, sleep, squat, stomp, twist*

Steps to Follow

1. Choose one child to be the leader and give him or her a piece of paper with six different actions, such as fall, freeze, run, sit, walk, and turn. Then turn on the music and have everyone begin to walk around the room. Have the leader call out one of the actions, which all of the children do until the leader calls out another action.

2. After the children are comfortable following these directions, give the same leader the second piece of paper with more actions on it.

3. If the children are listening and following the directions well, assign another child to be the leader.

Grandmother Elephant

Showing Leadership

Materials

- ❖ A copy of the strips and elephant on page 14 for each child (use heavy, white paper or card stock; if you do not wish to have the children color their elephant, use heavy, colored paper or colored card stock)
- ❖ Scissors
- ❖ Crayons or colored pencils
- ❖ Stapler
- ❖ Tape
- ❖ Double-stick tape or glue

Elephants can live for sixty-five years. Adult male elephants don't normally stay with their families but roam by themselves or with other males. Elephant mothers have one baby at a time and give birth every three or four years, always keeping a close eye on their babies and making sure they don't wander off.

The most important member of an elephant family is the grandmother. She leads the other elephants to watering holes and finds the easiest places to cross large rivers after it has rained. She knows where to find food, like melons, which elephants love to eat. She also leads them to grass, leaves, and twigs to eat. She knows where to find salt licks, where the earth is full of minerals that help elephants stay healthy.

If the grandmother elephant stops, all of the elephants stop. If she moves, the rest of the elephants move. If she senses danger, she will be the first to investigate and decide what to do. She might decide that she and the other elephants will run away. Or she might decide to charge. If she decides to charge, she will put her head down with her trunk tucked under her and charge at twenty-five miles per hour—faster than the fastest human being.

Steps to Follow

1. Color and cut out the elephant and the strips.
2. Tape the two strips together, forming one long strip.
3. Double-stick tape or glue the elephant to the strip.
4. Staple the two ends of the strip together, making a headband for the children to wear.

Note: This activity carries over into all the hero stories that follow. A different animal represents each hero's character quality. You can either have the children keep adding animals to the strip they've already made or have them make a new strip for each animal.

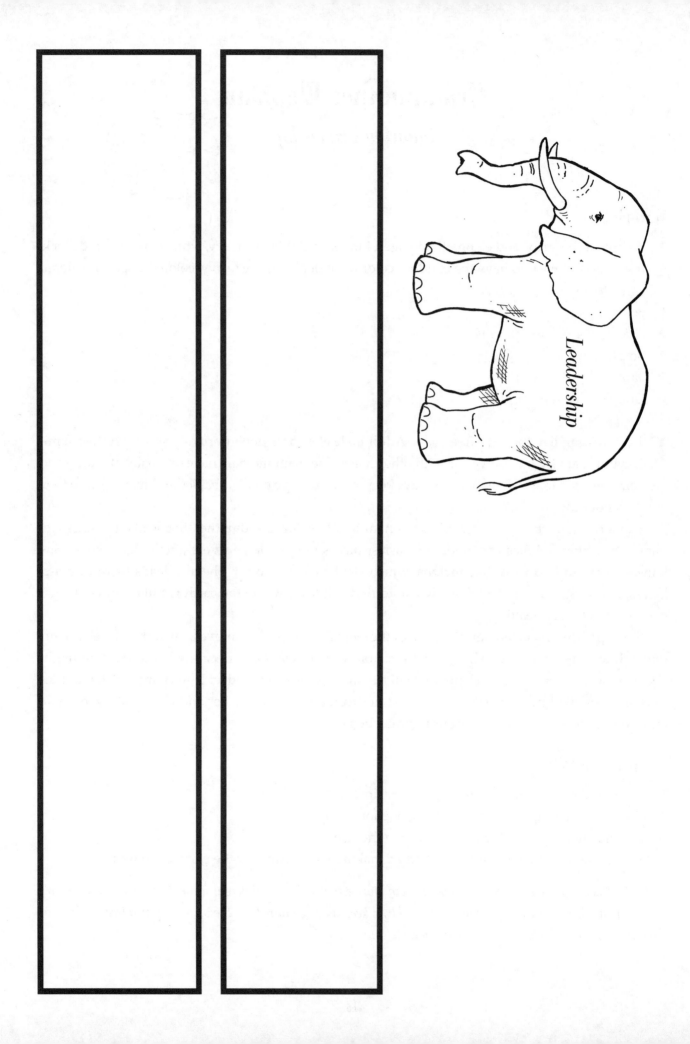

Leadership

Shoebox Activity for George Washington

Picture of George Washington

Materials

- ❖ One copy of the hat, circle, and half circle (on the following page) on white construction paper for each child
- ❖ One sheet of 8 ½ x 11 yellow construction paper for each child
- ❖ Six cotton balls for each child
- ❖ Small, quartered doily for each child
- ❖ Colored markers or colored pencils
- ❖ Double-stick tape or glue
- ❖ Scissors

Steps to Follow

1. Use markers or pencils to draw and color George's face (represented by the circle).

2. Cut out George's face.

3. Tape or glue the top part of George's face to the yellow construction paper, making sure the yellow paper is vertical. Place the face towards the upper middle part of the page, leaving room for the hat on top.

4. Color and cut out George's hat.

5. Tape or glue the hat onto George's head.

6. Color and cut out the half-circle for George's jacket.

7. Tape or glue the jacket beneath George's face.

8. Tape or glue a doily on the jacket right beneath George's chin to represent George's colonial ruffles; then tape or glue George's chin.

9. Cut six cotton balls in half.

10. Tape or glue the twelve pieces of cotton onto George's head to represent his wig.

11. Have the children put their George Washington picture in their shoeboxes. This will help them remember George and what a great leader he was to America.

16

Finding the 13 Stars

Materials

- ❖ One copy of the Fourth of July picnic picture on the following page for each child
- ❖ Crayons or colored pencils

Steps to Follow

1. Give each child a copy of the Fourth of July picnic picture. Explain to them, "The Declaration of Independence was signed on July 4, 1776. Today we still celebrate July 4th with parades and picnics."

2. Tell the children to find and color every one of the thirteen stars in the picture—the number of stars on the American flag at the time.

Stars and Stripes Kite

Here's a fun kite to make to celebrate July 4th, Independence Day.

Materials

- ❖ One white paper plate for each child
- ❖ Three two-foot long pieces of red, white, or blue yarn for each child
- ❖ Red and blue colored pencils or crayons or red and blue star stickers
- ❖ Black markers or crayons
- ❖ Hole punch
- ❖ Stapler or tape
- ❖ Scissors
- ❖ Red, white, and blue streamers

Steps to Follow

1. Cut out the center of a paper plate by first poking a hole in the middle, making sure not to cut into the rim. The center can be thrown away.

2. Decorate the plate by drawing red and blue stars or by using red and blue star stickers.

3. Take a hole punch and make three equally spaced holes around the plate about a half inch from the edge.

4. Tie a two-foot long piece of yarn to each hole.

5. Tie or knot the three strings together about six inches from each hole.

6. Staple or tape red, white, and blue streamers along the edges of the plate.

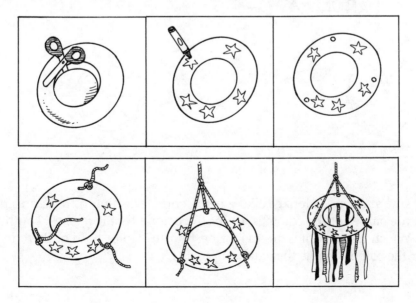

Map: George Washington

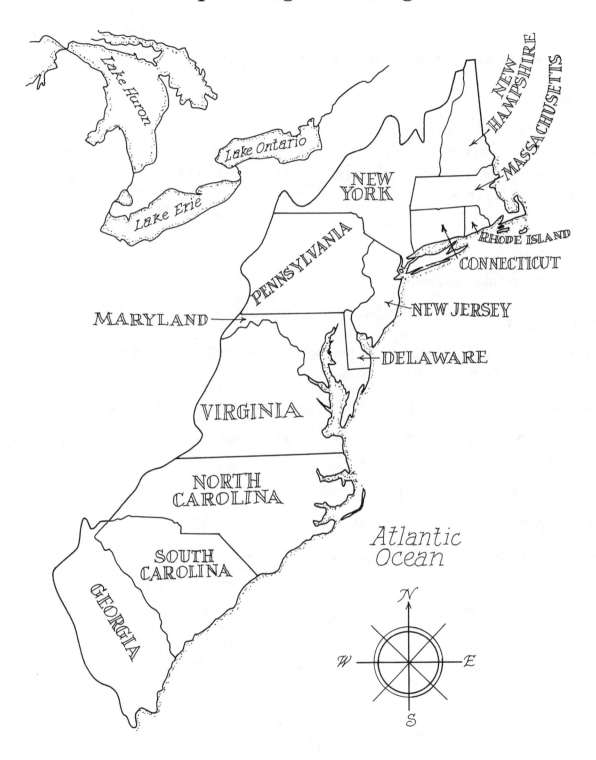

This is what America looked like when George Washington was president. Read the names of the colonies. Color the colony that is farthest south blue. Which two colonies are the farthest north? Color both of them red. Color the colony that is the smallest green.

The Flag of the United States

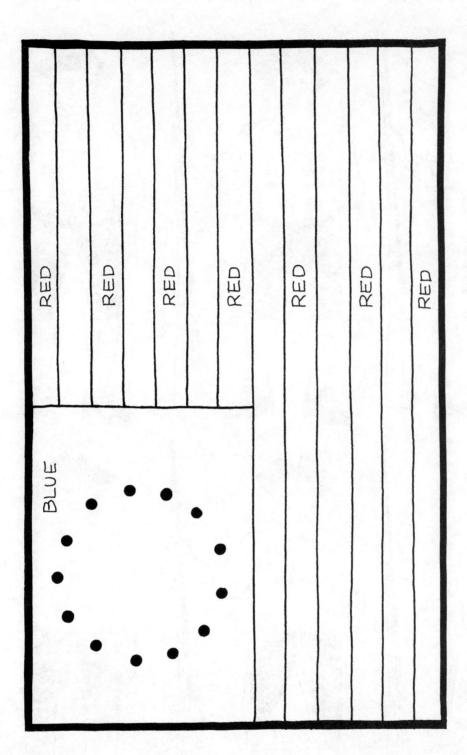

This is the flag that George Washington designed for the new country. The thirteen stars stand for the thirteen original colonies. Follow these directions to finish the flag:

1. Draw a star on each dot.
2. Color the flag red and blue where indicated. Leave the other parts white.
3. Cut out the flag and tape or staple it to a plastic straw.

George Washington Quiz

Color the Continental soldiers whose facts are correct.
Draw a big X over the ones whose facts are incorrect.

When young, George joined the British army to fight against the French.

The British were called "yellow coats."

The British hired soldiers from Spain to help them fight.

George's men were called "patriots."

In 1881 the British surrendered.

George became the first American president.

Fun with Rhyme

It's your turn to be a poet. See if you can fill in the correct word inside each Continental soldier without looking at your book on George Washington. Hint: The word rhymes with the last word in the second line.

He grew into a sturdy man,
   tall and athletic too.
And soon his childhood dream to fight
   with British troops came _____.

Word Bank
trees
retreated
true
hat
sight
more

These British "redcoats" all held muskets
   gleaming in the light,
and all were unaware an ambush
   was just out of _____.

The redcoats—easy targets—made
   George beg the general, "Please!
Allow the men to scatter, sir,
   behind the rocks and _____."

"That's not the British way," he said,
   and soon they were defeated.
Two horses that George rode were killed
   before they all _____.

He got back to the British camp
   and noticed as he sat
four bullet holes were in his coat
   and one was in his _____!

In New York harbor British warships
   landed troops on shore.
The men George led, called "patriots,"
   were pushed back more and _____.

George Washington Crossword Puzzle

Word Bank

thirteen

musket

Great Britain*

redcoats

patriots

general

Hessians

Independence

France

eight

*No space in crossword

Across

3. George's final rank in the military.
6. The country that joined America to help her win against Great Britain.
8. The name of German soldiers the British hired to help them.
9. The number of colonies ruled by Great Britain in 1740.
10. British soldiers were called _ _ _ _ _ _ _ _.

Down

1. In 1776 the colonists went to war with what country?
2. The Declaration of _ _ _ _ _ _ _ _ _ _ _ _.
4. The colonists were called _ _ _ _ _ _ _ _.
5. The number of years George Washington was president.
7. A shoulder gun the British used against the French.

Meriwether Lewis: Journey Across America

Meriwether Lewis Song

Meriwether Lewis led a team with William Clark. He faced great dangers and took risks to map out new landmarks.

He hiked and climbed, explored and paddled, finding brand new routes so those who crossed America could find their way about.

The journey, the journey, brave Meriwether journeyed past Indians and buffalo, wild rapids and long bows.

The journey, the journey, brave Meriwether journeyed. He found a land and water route no one had known about.

The Good Character Quality
of Meriwether Lewis

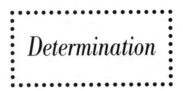

Determination

Definition of Determination: Doing all you can to achieve your goals despite difficulties.

Steps to Follow

1. Introduce the character quality of determination, which describes Meriwether, and discuss its meaning with the children.

2. Ask the children, "How did Meriwether show determination in his life through his words or actions?"
    - ❖ He helped deliver soldiers' pay while braving the wild frontier.
    - ❖ He fought strong currents and debris in both the Mississippi and Missouri Rivers.
    - ❖ He had to lug canoes to the top of the "Great Falls," and the route was filled with thorns, rocks, wolves, ferocious bears, and deadly rattlesnakes.
    - ❖ He struggled upriver through sweltering summer heat.
    - ❖ He climbed across a mountain range that was slippery and steep, and fought through icy sleet.
    - ❖ He had to navigate the dangerous Columbia River as his canoe pitched and rolled and thumped against jagged rocks and boulders.

3. Have the children sing the character song "We Will Be Determined" on page 29. (This song is sung to the tune of "Do Your Ears Hang Low?" If you have the CD for Meriwether Lewis, you can have the children follow or sing along with this song. At the end of the CD, there is a solo piano accompaniment that the children can sing along with as well.)

Meriwether Lewis Character Song

We Will Be Determined

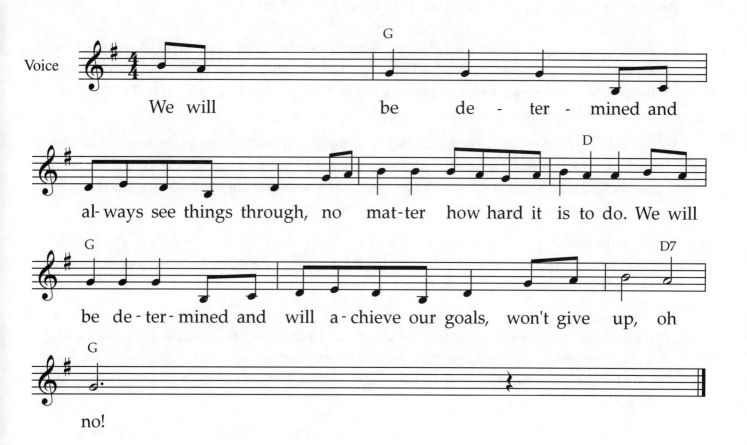

Voice

We will   be   de - ter - mined and

al-ways see things through,   no   mat-ter   how hard it   is to do. We will

be de-ter-mined and   will a-chieve our goals,   won't give   up,   oh

no!

Character Activity for Meriwether Lewis
An Imaginary Journey Across America

Read and act out the following imaginary journey with the children.

1. We're going to go on an imaginary journey with Meriwether Lewis. I'm Meriwether and you're my team. First, let's get in our boat and go up the Missouri River. Even though our boat has sails, the river's currents are stronger. We're going to have to take our oars and row really hard. Let's row. Wow! This is hard work.

2. Not only are there strong currents, but there also are unseen sandbars ahead that our boat can get stuck on. That means everybody out! We're going to have to pull the boat behind us. Start pulling! Is this ever exhausting! I'm glad you're all young and strong. Let's sing the character song "We Will be Determined."

3. Okay, it's getting toward evening, so we need to pull our boat ashore. Now let's go and explore. What is that? Why, it's two curious animals I've never seen before. What should we name them? How about "badger" and "coyote"?

4. Now we're in the Great Plains. Don't you love the open spaces? And look! I see some buffalo in the distance. And there are some Indians called the Mandan. They're asking us to go on a buffalo hunt. Do we have any volunteers to be horses? Great. Everyone else get on a horse and let's go. I see buffalo. Get your bows and arrows ready to shoot. Did anyone get a buffalo? Great. That was fun.

5. Let's get in our canoes and keep traveling. Stop. What's that? I hear a rumbling sound. What do you think it is? Why, it's five waterfalls, twelve miles long. We're going to have to carry our canoe up to the very top. This is going to be very tough—let's get started. Together, let's carry our canoe over our heads. Here we go. One, two, three, up over our heads. Be careful as you go over the rocks and thorns. Ouch! Those rocks and thorns really hurt!

6. Let's get back in our canoe now and go upriver. It's awfully hot. Look! There are some fleet-footed mountain sheep in the distance. Let's all wave to them.

7. Now we've come to the Rocky Mountains. I've managed to trade some supplies for some horses to get over them. So let's get out of our canoe. Some of you will have to be horses again so the rest of us can ride across the Rockies. So who's willing to be horses this time? Okay, let's get on our horses and go up the mountain range. It's so slippery and steep and the wind is so strong, it's really tough going. Now we're even heading into some icy sleet.

8. Let's keep going. Whew! We've finally made it to the other side. Look! The Columbia River is right ahead of us and there are lots of rapids! Let's get into another canoe and try to brave the

waters. Watch out! Our canoe is pitching and rolling, so try not to fall overboard. And be careful—our canoe is thumping against some rocks. Hold on! That was close. I'm feeling a bit seasick. How about you?

9. Let's get our canoe to shore now and start walking.

10. Look over there! It's the Pacific Ocean! I see some whales and dolphins swimming. Let's sink our feet in the sand and then in the water. We made it. What an adventure we've had.

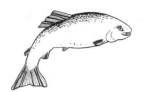

The Salmon

Showing Determination

Materials

- ❖ A copy of the strips and salmon on page 33 for each child (use heavy white paper or card stock; if you do not wish to have the children color the salmon, use heavy colored paper or colored card stock)
- ❖ Scissors
- ❖ Crayons or colored pencils
- ❖ Stapler
- ❖ Tape
- ❖ Double-stick tape or glue

Baby salmon start their lives in freshwater streams and then travel out to the ocean, staying there for three or four years. Now grown up, the salmon return to the streams where they were born. As they begin their journey upstream, they must overcome many obstacles, often leaping three to five feet up the side of a waterfall in order to get over the top. The salmon must also jump many feet out of the water in order to get over rushing rapids, dams, or giant rocks. Sometimes they must make several attempts to get over these obstacles.

The salmon travel as far as 25 miles a day to return to the place of their birth, often hundreds of miles away. Once they start, there is no turning back. They go without food, and they rely on the rays of the moon and the sun to know which way their home is.

It takes great determination for the salmon to make the long journey upriver, fighting the currents and other treacherous objects. It takes them as long as six months to arrive at their destination. Once the salmon get there, the female salmon lay their eggs. Then all the tired adults return downriver, having reached the end of their lives and having accomplished their mission to create healthy offspring.

Steps to Follow

1. Color and cut out the salmon and the strips.
2. Tape the two strips together, forming one long strip.
3. Double-stick tape or glue the salmon to the strip.
4. Staple the two ends of the strip together, making a headband for the children to wear.

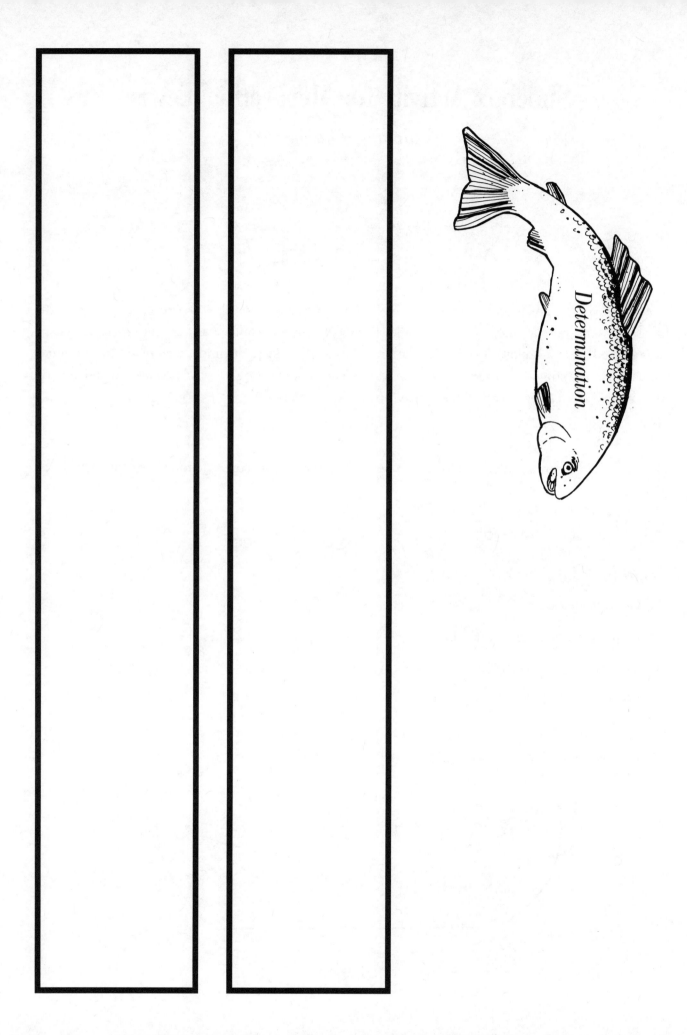

Determination

Shoebox Activity for Meriwether Lewis

Making a Canoe

American Indians used the canoe to travel on water. Some canoes held just one person, and others could hold as many as sixty people. The most common canoe was the dugout canoe, which was carved from a hollowed-out tree. The bullboat, another kind of canoe, was made from animal skins that were stretched around a wooden frame. The people riding in the canoe used wooden paddles carved from trees to propel the canoe through the water.

Materials

❖ Copy of the canoe pattern on the next page traced onto white construction paper for each child
❖ Stapler
❖ Scissors
❖ Crayons or colored pencils

Steps to Follow

1. Cut out the canoe.

2. Fold the canoe on the dotted line.

3. Decorate the canoe with animals, bows and arrows, trees, etc.

4. Staple the sides of the canoe shut.

5. Have the children put the canoe inside their shoeboxes with their other keepsakes. This will remind them of the important explorations of Meriwether Lewis.

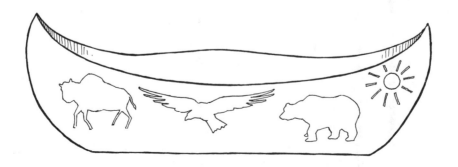

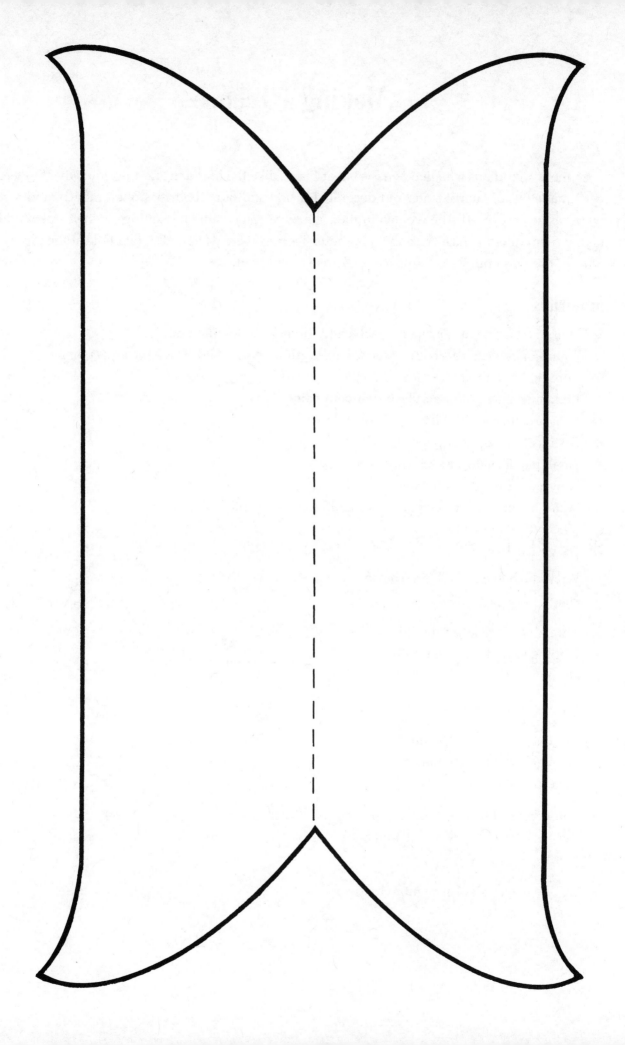

Making a Teepee

American Indians who lived on the Great Plains, like the Mandan and the Sioux, lived in teepees made out of animal skins and decorated inside and out. The tribes often moved, and teepees were easy to transport. The women in the tribe were responsible for setting up the teepees and for taking them down, which took about an hour. Teepees were designed with a hole at the top so that when a fire was built inside, smoke would rise up and out.

Materials

- ❖ Half of a large flour tortilla for each child (do not use low-fat ones)
- ❖ Four bamboo skewers cut to 7 inches in length for each child (leave the ends pointed)
- ❖ Three colored toothpicks for each child
- ❖ Red, blue, and yellow acrylic or tempera paint
- ❖ Paintbrush for each child
- ❖ Disinfecting wipes or paper towels
- ❖ Small paper plate for each child
- ❖ Newspaper to cover the table
- ❖ Water in small plastic cups for each child to rinse paintbrushes

Steps to Follow

1. Wrap the halved tortilla into a cone shape.

2. Thread toothpicks through the overlapping seam to hold the tortilla closed.

3. Put the teepee on a paper plate.

4. Place three skewers (pointed end up) through the small circular opening at the top of the teepee.

5. Paint colorful pictures and designs on the outside with acrylic or tempera paint.

6. Let the teepee sit over night to harden.

Sneak-Up Game

Explorers and hunters needed sharp ears and quiet feet. Here's a game to test each child's skills in these areas.

Materials

❖ Blindfold
❖ 3 wooden rulers or sticks

Steps to Follow

1. Choose one child to be the explorer or hunter, and have the child sit on his or her knees in the center of a large circle of children. Blindfold the child, making sure his or her ears are not covered.

2. Place the rulers or sticks in a row one foot from the explorer's knees.

3. Have the other children surrounding the explorer be wood gatherers. The teacher will silently point to a child and say, "Wood gatherers, we need wood!"

4. The chosen child will try to take one of the sticks without being heard. If the explorer hears the gatherer, he may reach out and tag the person. If the gatherer gets caught, he or she must sit back down. If the gatherer successfully sneaks away with the wood, he or she is the new explorer.

5. Explorers also may be changed after the three sticks have been taken.

Map: Meriwether Lewis

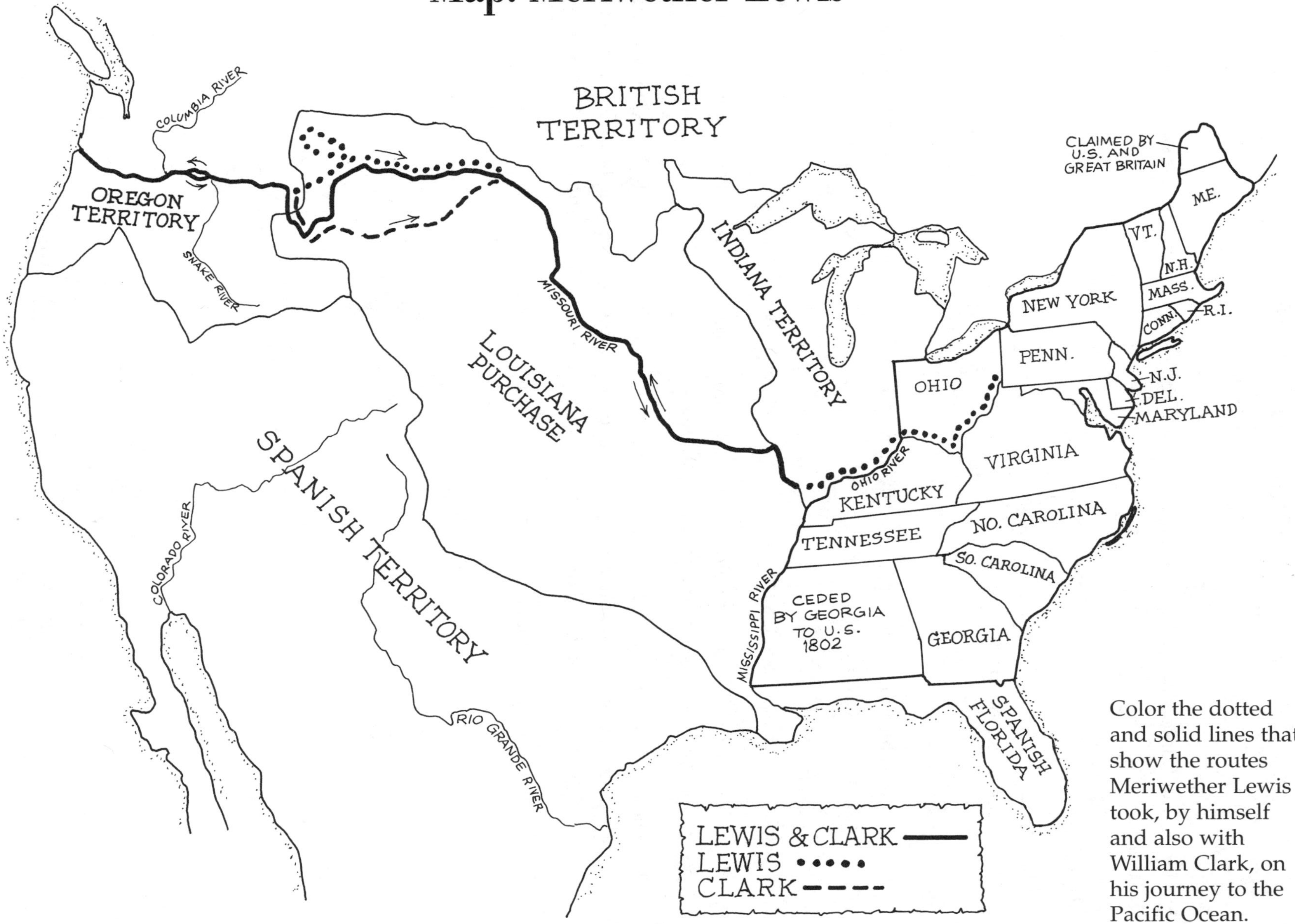

Color the dotted and solid lines that show the routes Meriwether Lewis took, by himself and also with William Clark, on his journey to the Pacific Ocean.

CLAIMED BY U.S. AND GREAT BRITAIN

ME.

VT.

N.H.

MASS.

CONN.

R.I.

N.J.

DEL.

MARYLAND

NEW YORK

PENN.

OHIO

VIRGINIA

NO. CAROLINA

SO. CAROLINA

GEORGIA

SPANISH FLORIDA

KENTUCKY

TENNESSEE

CEDED BY GEORGIA TO U.S. 1802

OHIO RIVER

MISSISSIPPI RIVER

INDIANA TERRITORY

BRITISH TERRITORY

LOUISIANA PURCHASE

MISSOURI RIVER

SPANISH TERRITORY

RIO GRANDE RIVER

COLORADO RIVER

SNAKE RIVER

COLUMBIA RIVER

OREGON TERRITORY

————	LEWIS & CLARK
••••••	LEWIS
– – – –	CLARK

Fifteen-Star Flag of the United States

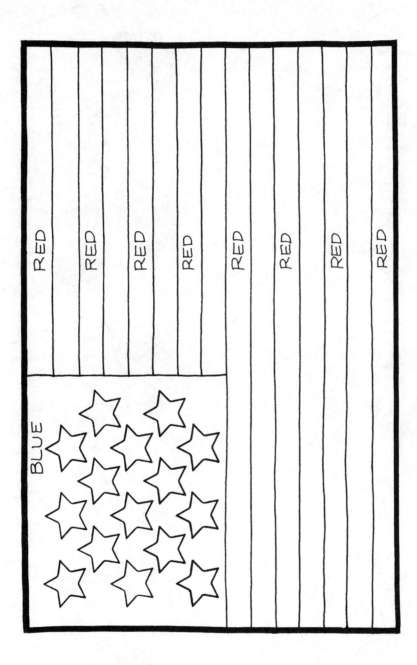

The second American flag, flown until 1818, had fifteen stars and fifteen stripes. This was America's flag when Francis Scott Key wrote "The Star Spangled Banner" in 1814. Color the flag blue and red where indicated.

Meriwether Lewis Quiz

Color the buffalo whose facts are correct.
Draw a big X over the ones whose facts are incorrect.

As a child, Meriwether did not like to be outdoors.

Meriwether began his journey west in 1903.

Meriwether's co-leader on his team out West was William Clark.

Meriwether traded with the Shoshone for thirty horses.

Meriwether saw two new animals: a squirrel and a cat.

The Columbia River had smooth waters and was easy to navigate.

The Mandan Indians took Meriwether and his team on a buffalo hunt.

Meriwether and his team never made it to the Pacific Ocean.

Getting Meriwether and his team across the waterfalls was easy.

Meriwether discovered a way by land and water to the Pacific Ocean.

Fun with Rhyme

It's your turn to be a poet. See if you can fill in the correct word inside each buffalo without looking at your book on Meriwether Lewis. Hint: The word rhymes with the last word in the second line.

He and his family left their cabin
     on a moonless night
and hid out in the forest, hoping
     they'd not have to

Word Bank
heat
through
hand
there
fight
see

When Meriwether got the job,
     he galloped over land
with money in his saddlebags,
     reins firmly in his

They left by boat in summertime
     in eighteen hundred three.
They carried food and things to trade
     with Indians they'd

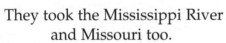

They took the Mississippi River
     and Missouri too.
They fought strong currents and debris,
     determined to get

The chiefs wore feathered headbands; their
     musicians kept a beat
with drums and deer-hoof rattles in
     the stifling summer

A few weeks later, smells of salt
     hung strongly in the air.
One man let out a holler of
     delight: "Look over

Meriwether Lewis Crossword Puzzle

Word Bank

canoe

coyote

Mississippi

Mandan

buffalo

teepee

Great Falls*

Clark

Jefferson

dolphin

*No space in crossword

Across

5. Five waterfalls that stretch twelve miles long.
7. A dwelling of certain American Indians.
8. A river Meriwether and his team took.
10. The name of an Indian tribe.

Down

1. Meriwether saw large herds of _ _ _ _ _ _ _.
2. An animal Meriwether had never seen before.
3. The name of the president who asked Meriwether to lead an exploration team.
4. Captain William _ _ _ _ _.
6. A marine mammal found in the Pacific Ocean.
9. A light, slender boat with pointed ends made from trees or animal skins.

Clara Barton: Courage to Serve

Clara Barton Song

Clara Barton was a nurse who helped heal wounded men. The "Angel of the Battlefield," she gave great care to them.

She made them slings and bandaged wounds and helped save many lives, and then she helped those hurt by floods and fires to survive.

The angel, the angel, yes, Clara was an angel. In war she nursed the injured men—fed and encouraged them.

The angel, the angel, yes, Clara was an angel to people hurt by war and loss. She gave us the Red Cross.

The Good Character Quality of Clara Barton

Caring

Definition of Caring: Being helpful and comforting to those in need.

Steps to Follow

1. Introduce the character quality of caring, which describes Clara, and discuss its meaning with the children.

2. Ask the children, "How did Clara show caring in her life through her words or actions?"
   - ❖ Clara, at only ten years old, cared for her brother for two years after he fell off a roof.
   - ❖ Clara cared for her students when she was a teacher by showing interest in what they did, like playing baseball.
   - ❖ Clara passed out bandages, blankets, and food when Union soldiers were attacked by Southerners.
   - ❖ Clara wrote letters to the soldiers' loved ones and put socks on their feet to keep them warm.
   - ❖ Clara risked her life by going to the front lines so she could rush life-saving care to the soldiers who were wounded, bandaging wounds and making slings for broken arms.
   - ❖ Clara brought lanterns so a doctor could work throughout the night and save the soldiers' lives.
   - ❖ Clara started the American Red Cross to help people during war and natural disasters.
   - ❖ When a hurricane hit a Carolina island, Clara taught the people how to grow edible and sweet crops, and she helped them make practical clothes from gowns that had been donated.

3. Look at the picture on the following page. Identify ways in which people are not being kind and caring. How can each situation be corrected?

4. Have the children sing the character song "We Will Be So Caring" on page 48. (This song is sung to the tune of "Do Your Ears Hang Low?" If you have the CD for Clara Barton, you can have the children follow or sing along with this song. At the end of the CD, there is a solo piano accompaniment that the children can sing along with as well.)

Clara Barton Character Song

We Will Be So Caring

Character Activity for Clara Barton

Making a Decorative Tissue Box

Here's a practical way to bless someone who is sick or sad.

Materials

- ❖ A cardboard tissue box full of tissues for each child
- ❖ Colored construction paper
- ❖ Colored tissue paper
- ❖ Feathers, beads, buttons, etc.
- ❖ Crayons or colored pencils
- ❖ Scissors
- ❖ Glue or double-stick tape

Steps to Follow

1. Have the children decorate a tissue box using colored construction paper, colored tissue paper, feathers, streamers, buttons, and crayons or colored pencils.

2. Tell the children to give the decorated tissue box to someone they know who is sick or sad.

 # The St. Bernard
Showing Caring

Materials

- ❖ A copy of the strips and picture of the St. Bernard on page 51 for each child (use heavy white paper or card stock; if you do not wish to have the children color the St. Bernard, use heavy colored paper or colored card stock)
- ❖ Scissors
- ❖ Crayons or colored pencils
- ❖ Stapler
- ❖ Tape
- ❖ Double-stick tape or glue

The St. Bernard is known around the world as the dog that rescues people. In 1750—more than 250 years ago—the dogs were well known for helping people on a dangerous route from Italy to Switzerland. On this mountainous route, people were often stranded because of robbers, avalanches, and terrible storms. Fortunately, the dogs' thick coats protected them against ice and snow. Their great sense of smell led them to people who had been buried in snow banks or avalanches. They even had the unique ability to sense when an avalanche was coming, which saved many lives.

St. Bernards have rescued more than two thousand travelers on one mountain pass that has been named after the dog. Today the dog is affectionately known as "The Saint" for its amazing contribution in helping to save lives. The St. Bernard is also very friendly and is a gentle family dog with a big heart.

Steps to Follow

1. Color and cut out the St. Bernard and the strips.
2. Tape the two strips together, forming one long strip.
3. Double-stick tape or glue the St. Bernard to the strip.
4. Staple the two ends of the strip together, making a headband for the children to wear.

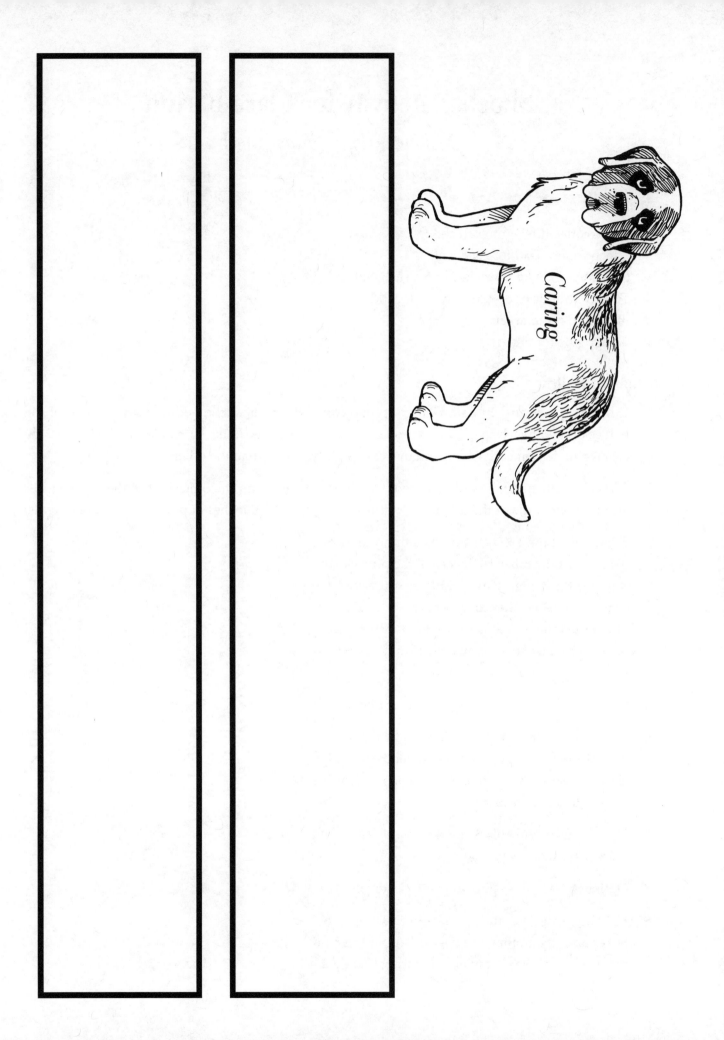

Caring

Shoebox Activity for Clara Barton
Making a Coffee Filter Angel

Materials

❖ Three coffee filters for each child
❖ ¾ inch round bead for each child
❖ One gold or silver pipe cleaner for each child
❖ Twenty strands of doll hair for each child
❖ Black and red markers
❖ Glitter glue (optional)

Steps to Follow

1. Cut the pipe cleaner in half. Gather up one coffee filter across the width and wind one of the halves of the pipe cleaner around it once to make the wings. Make sure at least 2 inches of pipe cleaner are left on both ends, with one end slightly longer than the other.

2. Cut about 20 strands of doll hair about six inches long. Wrap the other half of the pipe cleaner around the middle of the doll hair lengths leaving about 1 ½ inches of pipe cleaner at both ends.

3. Wind one of the 1 ½ inch lengths around to form a halo. Insert the other 1 ½ inches of the pipe cleaner through the center of the bead, then through the center of a coffee filter, and then through the center of another coffee filter. Bend a loop in the end of the pipe cleaner so the coffee filters and bead don't fall off.

4. Pull the coffee filters down to form the body.

5. Attach the wings to the body just below the bottom of the bead by wrapping the longer end of the pipe cleaner around the bead. Use both ends of the pipe cleaner to form the arms.

6. Draw a face with black markers and use a red marker for the cheeks.

7. Optional: Use glitter glue to paint the angel.

8. Have the children put the angel inside their shoeboxes with their other keepsakes. This will remind them of Clara's work and of how caring Clara was.

Hurricane Game

Hurricanes are powerful tropical storms that gather heat and energy from warm sea or ocean waters. Evaporation from the water increases their power.

Hurricanes rotate in a counter-clockwise direction around a central "eye" and have winds of at least 74 miles per hour. When they come onto land, the heavy rain, strong winds, and large waves can damage buildings, trees, and cars. The high waves are called a storm surge and are very dangerous. To be safe, people must stay away from the ocean during a hurricane warning.

Below is a fun hurricane game to play.

Materials

- ❖ The hut on the following page copied onto white construction paper for each child
- ❖ Table
- ❖ Rolled up newspaper
- ❖ Crayons or colored pencils
- ❖ Black marker
- ❖ Masking tape

Steps to Follow

1. Have each child color and cut out their tropical island hut.

2. While the children are coloring, place a strip of masking tape on the table in front of each child.

3. Assign each child a number and have them write that number on their piece of tape with a black marker. Then have each child write that same number on the back of their individual huts.

4. Tell the children, "A hurricane is coming!"

5. Have the children say, "Wooooooo!" Then take a rolled up newspaper and simulate a hurricane, swishing all the huts off the table in all directions.

6. Then say, "The hurricane has swept your huts away. Where did they go? I want you to find your hut and return it to your number on the table. One, two, three, GO!"

7. On the word "GO," have the children try to find their huts and bring them back to the table. The first child back to his or her spot wins the game.

Map: Clara Barton

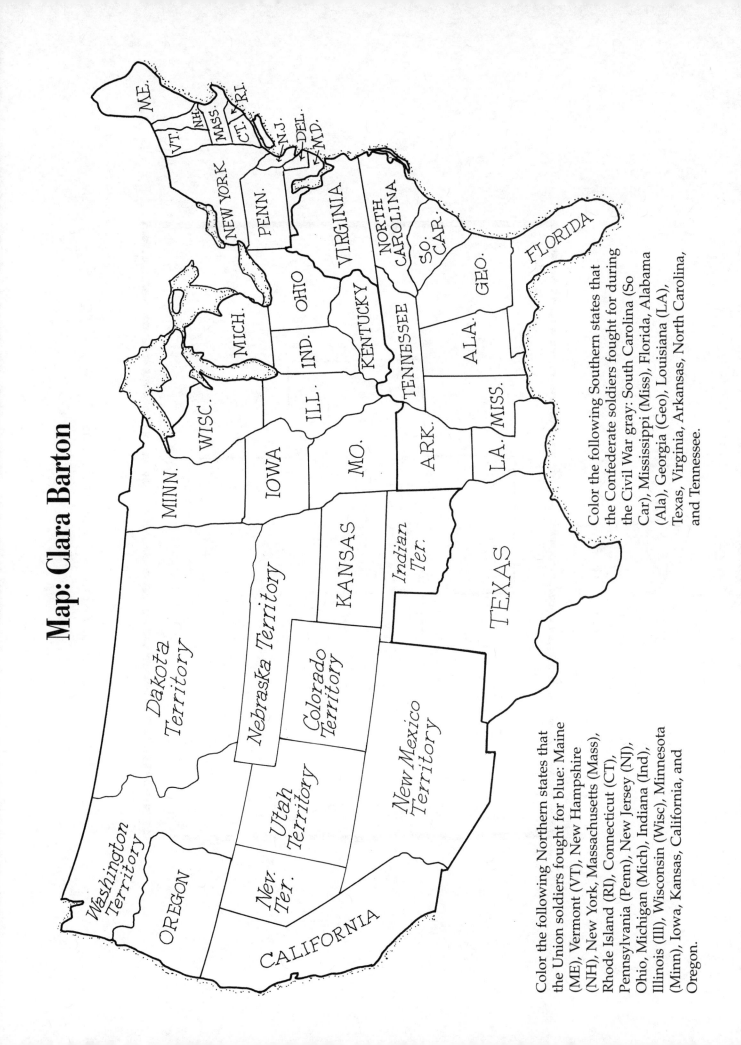

Color the following Northern states that the Union soldiers fought for blue: Maine (ME), Vermont (VT), New Hampshire (NH), New York, Massachusetts (Mass), Rhode Island (RI), Connecticut (CT), Pennsylvania (Penn), New Jersey (NJ), Ohio, Michigan (Mich), Indiana (Ind), Illinois (Ill), Wisconsin (Wisc), Minnesota (Minn), Iowa, Kansas, California, and Oregon.

Color the following Southern states that the Confederate soldiers fought for during the Civil War gray: South Carolina (So Car), Mississippi (Miss), Florida, Alabama (Ala), Georgia (Geo), Louisiana (LA), Texas, Virginia, Arkansas, North Carolina, and Tennessee.

Red Cross Flag

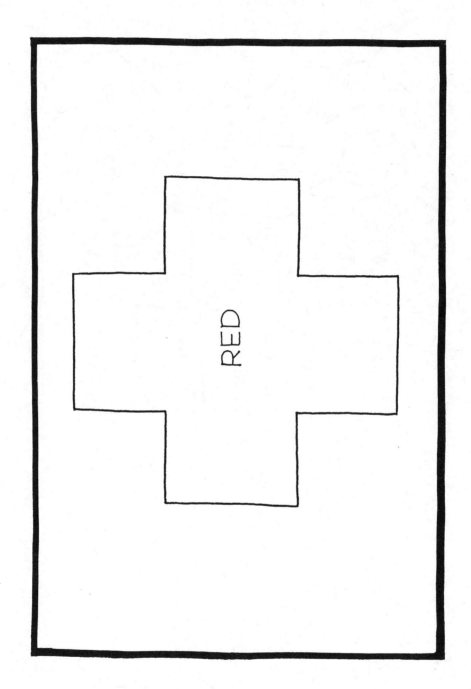

RED

Color the Red Cross flag red where indicated.

Clara Barton Quiz

Color the Red Cross flags whose facts are correct.
Draw a big X over the ones whose facts are incorrect.

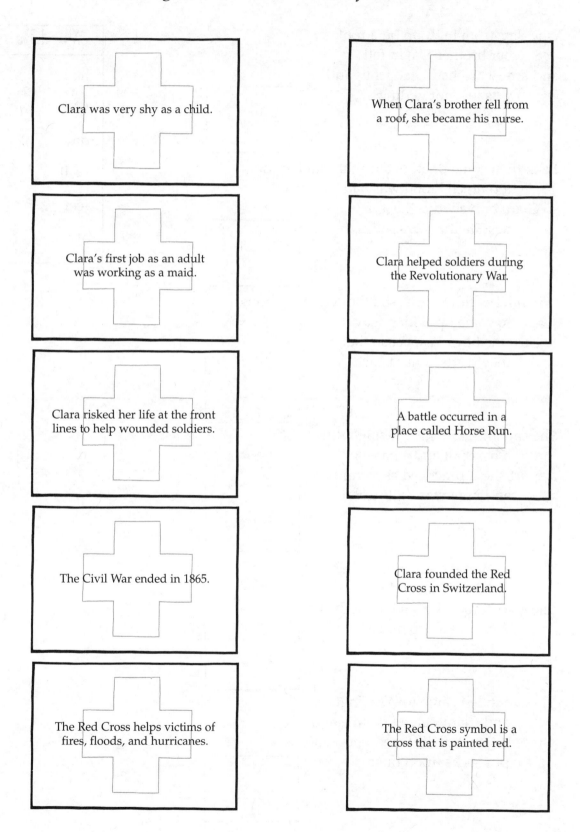

Clara was very shy as a child.

When Clara's brother fell from a roof, she became his nurse.

Clara's first job as an adult was working as a maid.

Clara helped soldiers during the Revolutionary War.

Clara risked her life at the front lines to help wounded soldiers.

A battle occurred in a place called Horse Run.

The Civil War ended in 1865.

Clara founded the Red Cross in Switzerland.

The Red Cross helps victims of fires, floods, and hurricanes.

The Red Cross symbol is a cross that is painted red.

Fun with Rhyme

It's your turn to be a poet. See if you can fill in the correct word inside each Red Cross flag without looking at your book on Clara Barton. Hint: The word rhymes with the last word in the second line.

One day, from high up on a roof,
    her brother David fell
and afterward had headaches and
    was just not getting

Word Bank
had
fun
day
well
feet
at

Back then some doctors thought that having
    too much blood was bad,
so Clara bravely did the job
    despite the fears she

When lunchtime came, she thought and thought
    to come up with a way
to earn the boys' respect so that
    they'd study hard each

She saw the students playing with
    a baseball and a bat—
a sport she'd practiced as a child
    and now was quite good

The boys, impressed, invited her
    to hit the ball and run.
She raced around from base to base;
    they all had so much

The wounded came to Washington,
    and Clara helped them eat,
wrote letters to their loved ones, and
    put socks upon their

Clara Barton Crossword Puzzle

Word Bank

Barton

Massachusetts

leech

Lincoln

American

Bull

Confederate

Union

Virginia

Antietam

Across

3. _ _ _ _ Run.
5. Name of the Northern army.
6. A dark and slimy creature that was used on sick people.
7. Clara founded the _ _ _ _ _ _ _ _ Red Cross.
9. Name of the Southern army.
10. Clara _ _ _ _ _ _ .

Down

1. A Southern state during the Civil War.
2. Name of the state Clara grew up in.
4. Name of the U.S. President during the Civil War.
8. A place in Maryland where a battle occurred.

George Washington Carver: America's Scientist

George Washington Carver Song

George Carver loved the outside world—loved frogs and plants and weeds. He studied hard so he could help the farmers with their needs.

He chose to use his clever mind and chose to use his time inventing things as Mister Peanut Man to bless mankind.

The peanut, the peanut, George used the little peanut to make things others had not tried—shampoo, cream, ink, and dye.

The peanut, the peanut, George used the little peanut. His education made him free to work creatively.

The Good Character Quality
of George Washington Carver

Creativeness

Definition of Creativeness: The ability to make or design something new through the use of imaginative skill.

Steps to Follow

1. Introduce the character quality of creativeness, which describes George, and discuss its meaning with the children.

2. Ask the children, "How did George show creativeness in his life through his words or actions?"
    ❖ He created many different peanut products like ink, milk, facial cream, shampoo, cereals, fruit punch, coffee, and dye.

3. Have the children sing the character song "We Will Be Creative" on page 65. (This song is sung to the tune of "Do Your Ears Hang Low?" If you have the CD for George Washington Carver, you can have the children follow or sing along with this song. At the end of the CD, there is a solo piano accompaniment that the children can sing along with as well.)

George Washington Carver Character Song

We Will Be Creative

We will be cre-a-tive and al-ways use our minds and im-

ag - i - na-tions; who knows what we'll find? We will be cre-a-tive, dis-

cov - er what we can with our heads and hands.

Character Activity for George Washington Carver
Creating with Peanut Butter Clay

George Washington Carver was very creative. We're going to make some edible peanut butter clay and see how many creative ways we can use it!

Ingredients

- ❖ 1 tsp. oil
- ❖ 1 cup peanut butter
- ❖ 2 ½ cups instant nonfat dry milk
- ❖ 1 cup honey
- ❖ Measuring cup
- ❖ Mixing bowl and spoon
- ❖ Plastic utensils
- ❖ Waxed paper
- ❖ Optional: Raisins, dry cereal, nuts, candy beads, or chocolate chips for decorating and creating

Steps to Follow (for the teacher)

Make the following recipe and refrigerate for one hour before class begins:

1. Swirl 1 teaspoon of oil in a measuring cup to avoid sticking.
2. Measure 1 cup of peanut butter and 1 cup of honey and mix together in a bowl.
3. Add 2 ½ cups of instant nonfat dry milk and mix together with the peanut butter and honey until it feels like soft dough.
4. Refrigerate the dough for 1 hour.

Steps to Follow (for the children)

1. Give each child a piece of waxed paper and some peanut butter "clay."
2. Have the children shape their dough into their own creations.
3. If desired, add raisins, dry cereal, nuts, and chocolate chips to make eyes, nose, ears, wings, feet, and so on.
4. Chill in the refrigerator again and then eat.

Note: This recipe makes enough clay for four students. If time permits, have the children make their own clay; if not, make the clay and refrigerate it ahead of time and let the children create with it.

Caution: Make sure that no one in your class has a peanut allergy. If they do, make sure it is okay with their parents to create with their peanut butter clay.

The Chimpanzee

Showing Creativeness

Materials

❖ Copy of the strips and picture of the chimpanzee on page 68 for each child (use heavy white paper or card stock; if you do not wish to have the children color the chimpanzee, use heavy colored paper or colored card stock)

❖ Scissors

❖ Crayons or colored pencils

❖ Stapler

❖ Tape

❖ Double-stick tape or glue

Chimpanzees communicate in many creative ways. In fact, scientists have found that chimpanzees use thirty-two different calls to communicate, such as various types of grunts, barks, screams, and hoots. They even use kisses and pats to communicate and can cry, whimper, and clack their teeth to express their emotions. They are constantly watching the faces of other chimpanzees to see how the others are feeling. When taught, they are able to learn American Sign Language and other languages that use symbols.

Young chimps are good at creating tools from different objects they find. They have a long, flexible great toe on their foot that is used like an additional thumb for climbing and grasping objects. They are very good at using sticks to dig out termites to eat and crumpled leaves to soak up water to drink.

Chimpanzees also creatively use plants as medicine to treat themselves when they become ill or injured.

Steps to Follow

1. Color and cut out the chimpanzee and the strips.
2. Tape the two strips together, forming one long strip.
3. Double-stick tape or glue the chimpanzee to the strip.
4. Staple the two ends of the strip together, making a headband for the children to wear.

Shoebox Activity for George Washington Carver
Making Peanut People

Materials

❖ Peanuts with shells
❖ Small snippets of fabric or colored construction paper
❖ Poster paint or tempera paint in different colors
❖ Paint brushes
❖ Small wiggle eyes
❖ Glue
❖ Pipe cleaners

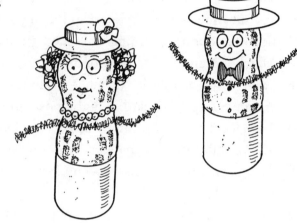

Steps to Follow

1. Choose several large peanuts in their shells.

2. Glue wiggle eyes on the peanuts.

3. Paint on the nose and mouth.

4. Cut out a small strip of cloth or construction paper about 1 inch wide by 2 inches long. Place glue on the bottom half of the peanut. Dress the peanut by placing fabric or construction paper around the bottom half of the peanut, pressing it firmly against the glue.

5. Glue bow ties, top hats, or bonnets from fabric or construction paper onto the peanuts.

6. Cut a pipe cleaner into 3-inch-long pieces. Wrap one piece around the middle of the peanut for arms.

7. Have the children put their peanut people in their shoeboxes to remind them of the creativity of George Washington Carver, who invented over 300 uses for the peanut!

Peanut Facts

Here are some interesting peanut facts:

❖ George Washington Carver discovered more than 300 uses for the peanut.

❖ The peanut is actually not a nut, but a legume related to beans and lentils.

❖ Peanuts are planted after the last frost in April or early May and take about five months from planting to harvesting.

❖ A mature peanut plant produces about 40 pods that then grow into peanuts.

❖ The peanut plant produces a small yellow flower.

❖ Peanuts flower above ground and then go underground until they reach maturity.

❖ In some countries, peanuts are called groundnuts.

❖ March is National Peanut Month.

❖ Four of the top candy bars made in America contain peanuts or peanut butter.

❖ Astronaut Alan Shepard brought a peanut with him to the moon.

❖ The world's largest peanut was 4 inches long.

❖ The peanut plant originated in South America.

❖ Two peanut farmers have been elected president of the United States: Thomas Jefferson and Jimmy Carter.

❖ Peanut butter is the leading use of peanuts in America.

❖ It takes 540 peanuts to make a 12-ounce jar of peanut butter.

❖ There are enough peanuts in one acre to make 30,000 peanut butter sandwiches.

❖ 89 percent of Americans eat peanut butter.

❖ The world's largest peanut butter factory churns out 250,000 jars of the tasty treat every day.

❖ Women and children generally prefer creamy peanut butter, while most men prefer chunky.

❖ People living on the East Coast generally prefer creamy peanut butter, while those on the West Coast prefer the crunchy style.

❖ 60 percent of people prefer creamy peanut butter over crunchy.

❖ November is Peanut Butter Lovers Month.

❖ Arachibutyrophobia is the fear of getting peanut butter stuck to the roof of your mouth.

❖ The average child will eat 1,500 peanut butter and jelly sandwiches before he or she graduates from high school.

❖ Americans eat enough peanut butter in a year to make more than 10 billion peanut butter and jelly sandwiches.

Map: George Washington Carver

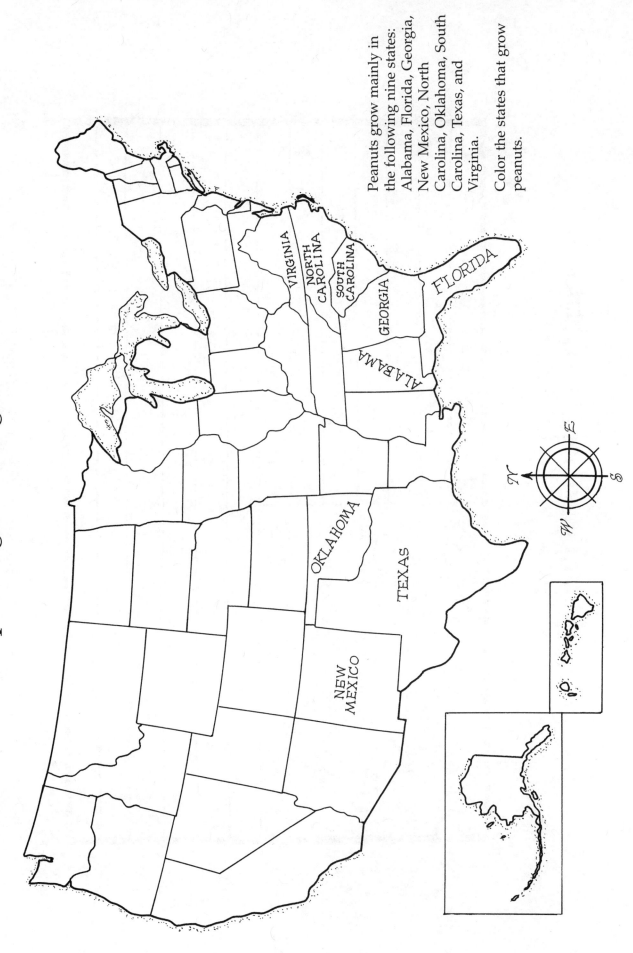

Peanuts grow mainly in the following nine states: Alabama, Florida, Georgia, New Mexico, North Carolina, Oklahoma, South Carolina, Texas, and Virginia.

Color the states that grow peanuts.

36-Star Flag of the United States

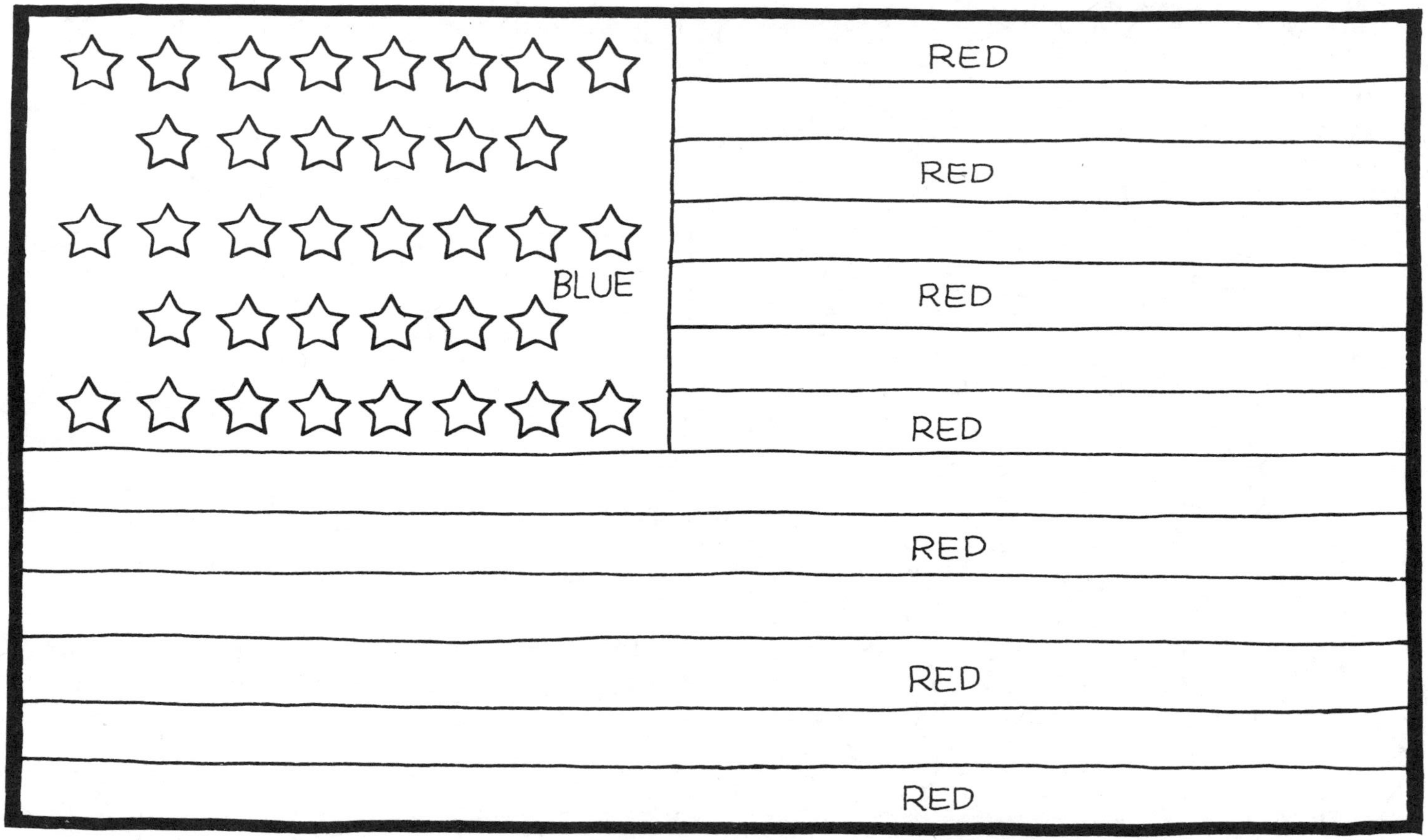

RED

RED

RED

RED

RED

RED

RED

BLUE

The American flag had thirty-six stars near the close of the Civil War, about the time that George Washington Carver was born. Today it has fifty. Color the flag red and blue where indicated. Leave the other parts white.

George Washington Carver Quiz

Color the peanuts whose facts are correct.
Draw a big X over the ones whose facts are incorrect.

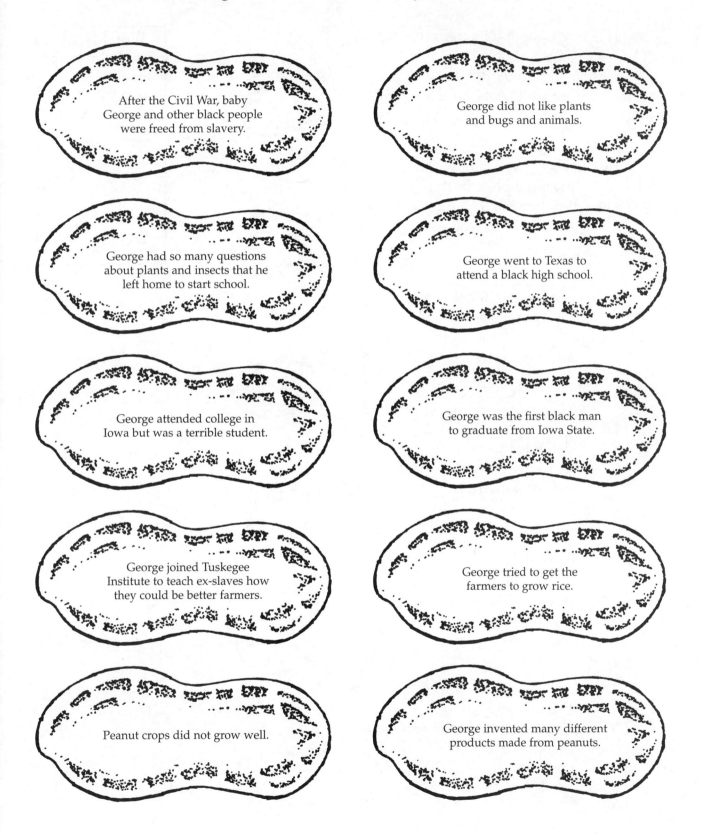

After the Civil War, baby George and other black people were freed from slavery.

George did not like plants and bugs and animals.

George had so many questions about plants and insects that he left home to start school.

George went to Texas to attend a black high school.

George attended college in Iowa but was a terrible student.

George was the first black man to graduate from Iowa State.

George joined Tuskegee Institute to teach ex-slaves how they could be better farmers.

George tried to get the farmers to grow rice.

Peanut crops did not grow well.

George invented many different products made from peanuts.

Fun with Rhyme

It's your turn to be a poet. See if you can fill in the correct word inside each peanut without looking at your book on George Washington Carver. Hint: The word rhymes with the last word in the second line.

This boy, George Carver, lived deep in
    Missouri on a farm.
He lost his mother during war
    but God kept him from

He did chores at a family's home
    to earn a place to stay.
They gave him his own Bible that
    he learned to read each

George had no money to replace
    his precious books and knew
he'd have to quit the school he loved
    and find some work to

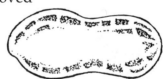

He took a train to college—
    delighted to be there.
An older woman met him with
    a most unfriendly

Six years went by before George heard
    about another place—
a college that he could attend
    regardless of his

The students secretly slipped dollar
    bills under his door.
These gifts touched George and made him feel
    accepted even

Word Bank
harm
glare
race
more
do
day

George Washington Carver Crossword Puzzle

Word Bank

Civil

Kansas

horticulture

beetle

cotton

peanut

shampoo

Edison

doctorate

Man

Across

2. The type of crop George convinced the farmers to grow.
4. The honorary degree George was awarded.
6. The kind of crop the boll weevil destroyed.
7. A soapy product made from peanuts.
10. The type of insect a boll weevil is.

Down

1. The State where George attended high school.
3. Something George studied in college.
5. The last name of the famous inventor who tried to employ George.
8. Mr. Peanut _ _ _.
9. The _ _ _ _ _ War.

Can You Name the Hero?

See if you can write the correct name of each hero in the space provided from the clues in each verse.

Can you name the hero who crossed the Delaware
    surprising Hessian soldiers to win a victory there?
Can you name the hero, the man who came to be
    the president who led with honor and humility?

His name was _____. He won a victory.

Can you name the hero who traveled with his team
    by river and by horse, over mountains and through streams?
Can you name the hero who bravely headed west
    because exploring was the thing at which he was the best?

His name was _____. He did explore the west.

Can you name the hero who showed how much she cared
    by helping wounded soldiers in battles everywhere?
Can you name the hero who shyness overcame?
    The "Angel of the Battlefield" became her brand-new name.

Her name was _____, an angel during war.

Can you name the hero who helped out many poor—
    teaching farmers how to grow crops better than before?
Can you name the hero so loved throughout the land
    that he was called affectionately "Mister Peanut Man?"

His name was _____, "Mister Peanut Man."

Note: This exercise can also be sung by following along on the companion CD. When the chorus is repeated the second time, the answers are included.

Answers to Questions

Answers to George Washington

George Washington Quiz: Correct Facts

- When young, George joined the British army to fight against the French.
- George's men were called "patriots."
- George became the first American president.

Fun with Rhyme

1. true
2. sight
3. trees
4. retreated
5. hat
6. more

Crossword

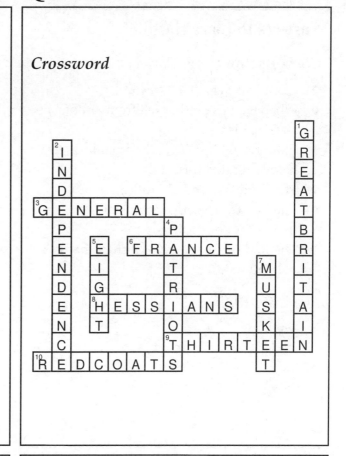

Answers to Meriwether Lewis

Meriwether Lewis Quiz: Correct Facts

- Meriwether's co-leader on his team out West was William Clark.
- Meriwether traded with the Shoshone for thirty horses.
- The Mandan Indians took Meriwether and his team on a buffalo hunt.
- Meriwether discovered a way by land and water to the Pacific Ocean.

Fun with Rhyme

1. fight
2. hand
3. see
4. through
5. heat
6. there

Crossword

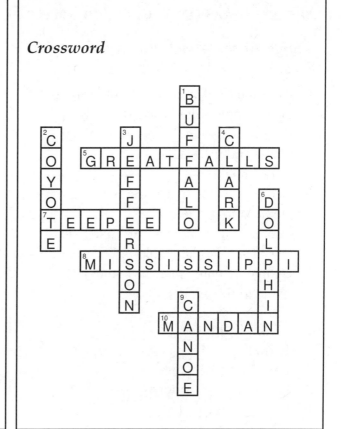

Answers to Clara Barton

Clara Barton Quiz: Correct Facts

- ❖ Clara was very shy as a child.
- ❖ When Clara's brother fell from a roof, she became his nurse.
- ❖ Clara risked her life at the front lines to help wounded soldiers.
- ❖ The Civil War ended in 1865.
- ❖ The Red Cross helps victims of fires, floods, and hurricanes.
- ❖ The Red Cross symbol is a cross that is painted red.

Fun with Rhyme

1. well
2. had
3. day
4. at
5. fun
6. feet

Crossword

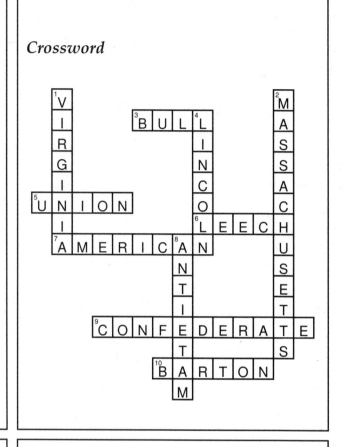

Answers to George Washington Carver

George Washington Carver Quiz: Correct Facts

- ❖ After the Civil War, baby George and other black people were freed from slavery.
- ❖ George had so many questions about plants and insects that he left home to start school.
- ❖ George was the first black man to graduate from Iowa State.
- ❖ George joined Tuskegee Institute to teach ex-slaves how they could be better farmers.
- ❖ George invented many different products made from peanuts.

Fun with Rhyme

1. harm
2. day
3. do
4. glare
5. race
6. more

Crossword

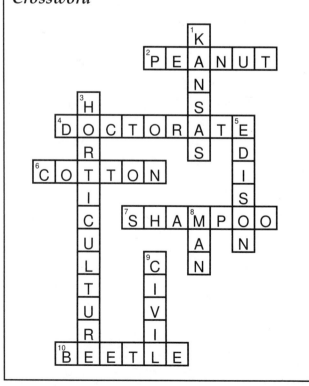

Syllabus

This syllabus lays out two options for a weekly lesson. By following the lesson plans for forty-five minute classes, you will be able to complete all the activities presented. Thirty-minute lessons cover most, but not all, of the activities.

Week 1

George Washington: 30-minute class

1. Read the book *George Washington: America's Patriot* (10 minutes).
2. Learn about the Good Character Quality of George Washington on page 10 and sing the Character Song "We Will Be Good Leaders" by listening to the companion CD and following along on page 11 (10 minutes).
3. Do the Character Activity on page 12 (10 minutes).
   Note: If the children finish early, let them color the George Washington Picture on page 7; otherwise, let them take it home to color.

George Washington: 45-minute class

1. Read the book *George Washington: America's Patriot*. Tell them to listen carefully because there will be a short quiz afterward (10 minutes).
2. Take the George Washington Quiz on page 22 (5 minutes).
3. Learn and sing the "George Washington Song" by listening to the companion CD and following along on page 9 (5 minutes).
4. Learn about the Good Character Quality of George Washington on page 10 and sing the Character Song "We Will Be Good Leaders" by listening to the companion CD and following along on page 11 (10 minutes).
5. Do the Character Activity on page 12 (10 minutes).
6. Find the 13 stars on pages 17–18 (5 minutes).
   Note: If the children finish early, let them color the George Washington Picture on page 7; otherwise, let them take it home to color.

Week 2

George Washington: 30-minute class

1. Learn and sing the "George Washington Song" by listening to the companion CD and following along on page 9 and/or the Character Song "We Will Be Good Leaders" on page 11 (5 minutes).
2. Do the Shoebox Activity on page 15 (25 minutes).
   Optional: While the children are making their craft, play the "George Washington Song" and "We Will Be Good Leaders" from the companion CD for them to listen to.

George Washington: 45-minute class

1. Learn about the grandmother elephant's leadership on page 13 and color and cut out the hat and elephant on page 14 (10 minutes).
2. Do Fun With Rhyme on page 23 (5 minutes).
3. Color and cut out the Flag on page 21 (5 minutes).
4. Do the Shoebox Activity on page 15 (25 minutes).
   Optional: While the children are making their craft, play the "George Washington Song" and "We Will Be Good Leaders" from the companion CD for them to listen to.

Week 3

Meriwether Lewis: 30-minute class

1. Read the book *Meriwether Lewis: Journey Across America* (10 minutes).
2. Learn about the Good Character Quality of Meriwether on page 28 and sing the Character Song "We Will Be Determined" by listening to the companion CD and following along on page 29 (10 minutes).
3. Do the Character Activity on pages 30–31 (10 minutes).

Meriwether Lewis: 45-minute class

1. Read the book *Meriwether Lewis: Journey Across America*. Tell them to listen carefully because there will be a short quiz afterward (10 minutes).
2. Take the Meriwether Lewis Quiz on page 40 (5 minutes).
3. Learn about the Good Character Quality of Meriwether on page 28 and sing the Character Song "We Will Be Determined" by listening to the companion CD and following along on page 29 (10 minutes).
4. Do the Character Activity on pages 30–31 (10 minutes).
5. Do the Shoebox Activity on page 34 (10 minutes).
   Optional: While the children are making their craft, play the "Meriwether Lewis Song" and "We Will Be Determined" from the companion CD for them to listen to.

Week 4

Meriwether Lewis: 30-minute class

1. Learn about and make a teepee on page 36 (30 minutes).
   Optional: While the children are making their craft, play the "Meriwether Lewis Song" and "We Will Be Determined" from the companion CD for them to listen to.
   Note: If the children finish early, let them color the Meriwether Lewis Picture on page 25; otherwise, let them take it home to color.

Meriwether Lewis: 45-minute class

1. Learn and sing the "Meriwether Lewis Song" on page 27 and/or the Character Song "We Will Be Determined" on page 29 (5 minutes).

2. Learn about the salmon's determination on page 32 and color and cut out the salmon on page 33 (10 minutes).
3. Learn about and make a teepee on page 36 (30 minutes).

   Optional: While the children are making their craft, play the "Meriwether Lewis Song" and "We Will Be Determined" from the companion CD for them to listen to.

   Note: If the children finish early, let them color the Meriwether Lewis Picture on page 25; otherwise, let them take it home to color.

Week 5

Clara Barton: 30-minute class

1. Read the book *Clara Barton: Courage to Serve*. Tell them to listen carefully because there will be a short quiz afterward (10 minutes).
2. Take the Clara Barton Quiz on page 57 (5 minutes).
3. Learn and sing the "Clara Barton Song" by listening to the companion CD and following along on page 45 (5 minutes).
4. Learn about the Good Character Quality of Clara on pages 46–47 and sing the Character Song "We Will Be So Caring" by listening to the companion CD and following along on page 48 (10 minutes).

   Note: If the children finish early, let them color the Clara Barton Picture on page 43; otherwise, let them take it home to color.

Clara Barton: 45-minute class

1. Read the book *Clara Barton: Courage to Serve* (10 minutes).
2. Learn about the Good Character Quality of Clara Barton on pages 46–47 and sing the Character Song "We Will Be So Caring" by listening to the companion CD and following along on page 48 (10 minutes).
3. Do the Character Activity for Clara on page 49 (25 minutes).

   Optional: While the children are making their craft, play the "Clara Barton Song" and "We Will Be So Caring" from the companion CD for them to listen to.

   Note: If the children finish early, let them color the Clara Barton Picture on page 43; otherwise, let them take it home to color.

Week 6

Clara Barton: 30-minute class

1. Review the "Clara Barton Song" by listening to the companion CD and following along on page 45 (5 minutes).
2. Do the Character Activity for Clara on page 49 (25 minutes).

   Optional: While the children are making their craft, play the "Clara Barton Song" and the Character Song "We Will Be So Caring" from the companion CD for them to listen to.

Clara Barton: 45-minute class

1. Learn and sing the "Clara Barton Song" by listening to the companion CD and following along on page 45 (5 minutes).
2. Review the Character Song "We Will Be So Caring" on page 48 (5 minutes).
3. Learn about the St. Bernard's care on page 50 and color and cut out the St. Bernard on page 51 (10 minutes).
4. Do Fun With Rhyme on page 58 (5 minutes).
5. Do the Shoebox Activity on page 52 (20 minutes).

Week 7

George Washington Carver: 30-minute class

1. Read the book *George Washington Carver: America's Scientist*. Tell them to listen carefully because there will be a short quiz afterward (10 minutes).
2. Take the George Washington Carver Quiz on page 73 (5 minutes).
3. Learn and sing the "George Washington Carver Song" by listening to the companion CD and following along on page 63 (5 minutes).
4. Learn about the Good Character Quality of George Washington Carver and sing the Character Song "We Will Be Creative" by listening to the companion CD and following along on page 65 (10 minutes).

   Note: If the children finish early, let them color the George Washington Carver Picture on page 61; otherwise, let them take it home to color.

George Washington Carver: 45-minute class

1. Read the book *George Washington Carver: America's Scientist* (10 minutes).
2. Learn about the Good Character Quality of George Washington Carver and sing the Character Song "We Will Be Creative" by listening to the companion CD and following along on page 65 (10 minutes).
3. Do the Character Activity for George Washington Carver on page 66 (25 minutes).

   Optional: While the children are creating with their peanut-butter clay, play the "George Washington Carver Song" and "We Will Be Creative" from the companion CD for them to listen to.

Week 8

George Washington Carver: 30-minute class

1. Review the "George Washington Carver Song" by listening to the companion CD and following along on page 63 (5 minutes).
2. Do the Character Activity for George Washington Carver on page 66 (25 minutes).

   Optional: While the children are creating with their peanut-butter, play the "George Washington Carver Song" and "We Will Be Creative" from the companion CD for them to listen to.

George Washington Carver: 45-minute class

1. Learn and sing the "George Washington Carver Song" by listening to the companion CD and following along on page 63 (5 minutes).
2. Learn about the chimpanzee's creativeness on page 67 and color and cut out the chimpanzee on page 68 (10 minutes).
3. Do the Map on page 71 (5 minutes).
4. Do the Flag on page 72 (5 minutes).
5. Do the Shoebox Activity on page 69 (20 minutes).
   Optional: While the children are making their craft, play the "George Washington Carver Song" and "We Will Be Creative" from the companion CD for them to listen to.

Week 9

George Washington: 30-minute class

1. Reread the book *George Washington: America's Patriot* (10 minutes).
2. Make the Stars and Stripes Kite on page 19 (20 minutes).
   Optional: While the children are making their craft, play the "George Washington Song" and "We Will Be Good Leaders" from the companion CD for them to listen to.

George Washington: 45-minute class

1. Reread the book *George Washington: America's Patriot* (10 minutes).
2. Work the Crossword Puzzle on page 24 (10 minutes).
3. Do the Map on page 20 (5 minutes).
4. Make the Stars and Stripes Kite on page 19 (20 minutes).
   Optional: While the children are making their craft, play the "George Washington Song" and "We Will Be Good Leaders" from the companion CD for them to listen to.

Week 10

Meriwether Lewis: 30-minute class

1. Reread the book *Meriwether Lewis: Journey Across America*. Tell them to listen carefully because there will be a short quiz afterward (10 minutes).
2. Take the Meriwether Lewis Quiz on page 40 (5 minutes).
3. Learn and sing the "Meriwether Lewis Song" by listening to the companion CD and following along on page 27 (5 minutes).
4. Do the Shoebox Activity on page 34 (10 minutes).
   Optional: While the children are making their craft, play the "Meriwether Lewis Song" and "We Will Be Determined" from the companion CD for them to listen to.

Meriwether Lewis: 45-minute class

1. Reread the book *Meriwether Lewis: Journey Across America* (10 minutes).

2. Work the Crossword Puzzle on page 42 (10 minutes).
3. Do Fun with Rhyme on page 41 (5 minutes).
4. Play a "Sneak Up" Game on page 37 (10 minutes).
5. Do the Map on page 38 (5 minutes).
6. Color the flag on page 39 (5 minutes).
    Optional: While the children are coloring, play the "Meriwether Lewis Song" and "We Will Be Determined" from the companion CD for them to listen to.

Week 11

Clara Barton: 30-minute class

1. Reread the book *Clara Barton: Courage to Serve* (10 minutes).
2. Do the Shoebox Activity on page 52 (20 minutes).

Clara Barton: 45-minute class

1. Reread the book *Clara Barton: Courage to Serve*. Tell them to listen carefully because there will be a short quiz afterward (10 minutes).
2. Take the Clara Barton Quiz on page 57 (5 minutes).
3. Do the Map on page 55 (8 minutes).
4. Do the Flag on page 56 (2 minutes).
5. Do the Hurricane Game on page 53 (10 minutes).
6. Work the Crossword Puzzle on page 59 (10 minutes).

Week 12

George Washington Carver: 30-minute class

1. Reread the book *George Washington Carver: America's Scientist* (10 minutes).
2. Do the Shoebox Activity on page 69 (20 minutes).
    Optional: While the children are making their craft, play the "George Washington Carver Song" and "We Will Be Creative" from the companion CD for them to listen to.

George Washington Carver: 45-minute class

1. Reread the book *George Washington Carver: America's Scientist*. Tell them to listen carefully because there will be a short quiz afterward (10 minutes).
2. Take the George Washington Carver Quiz on page 73 (5 minutes).
3. Review the "George Washington Carver Song" by listening to the companion CD and following along on page 63 and/or the Character Song "We Will Be Creative" on page 65 (5 minutes).
4. Do Fun with Rhyme on page 74 (5 minutes).
5. Work the Crossword Puzzle on page 75 (10 minutes).
6. Color the George Washington Carver picture on page 61 (10 minutes).
    Optional: While the children are coloring, play the "George Washington Carver Song" and "We Will Be Creative" from the companion CD for them to listen to.

Week 13

30-minute class

1. Sing the "Can You Name the Hero?" song by listening to the companion CD and following along on page 76 (5 minutes).
2. Read the definitions of the character traits on each of the Good Character Quality pages and see if the children can guess the trait and the name of the hero that the trait applies to (5 minutes).
3. Play the game "Who Am I?" Have each child pick the name of one of the four heroes from a basket and give a clue about who that hero is. Let the rest of the class try to guess who the hero is (10 minutes).
4. Have each child pick the name of one of the four heroes from a basket and draw a picture that makes others think of that hero, e.g., a canoe, a Red Cross symbol, a cannon, or peanut (10 minutes).

45-minute class

1. Sing the "Can You Name the Hero?" song by listening to the companion CD and following along on page 76 (5 minutes).
2. Read the definitions of the character traits on each of the Good Character Quality pages and see if the children can guess the trait and the name of the hero that the trait applies to (5 minutes).
3. Play the game "Who Am I?" Have each child pick the name of one of the four heroes from a basket and give a clue about who that hero is. Let the rest of the class try to guess who the hero is (10 minutes).
4. Have each child pick the name of one of the four heroes from a basket and draw a picture that makes others think of that hero, e.g., a canoe, a Red Cross symbol, a cannon, or peanut (10 minutes).
5. Tell who your favorite hero is and why (5 minutes).
6. Ask the children to pick their favorite songs and sing them (10 minutes).

Notes

Notes

Notes

Notes

Notes

Notes

Notes

Notes

Notes

Notes